Un

Our Life/
Our World

Contents

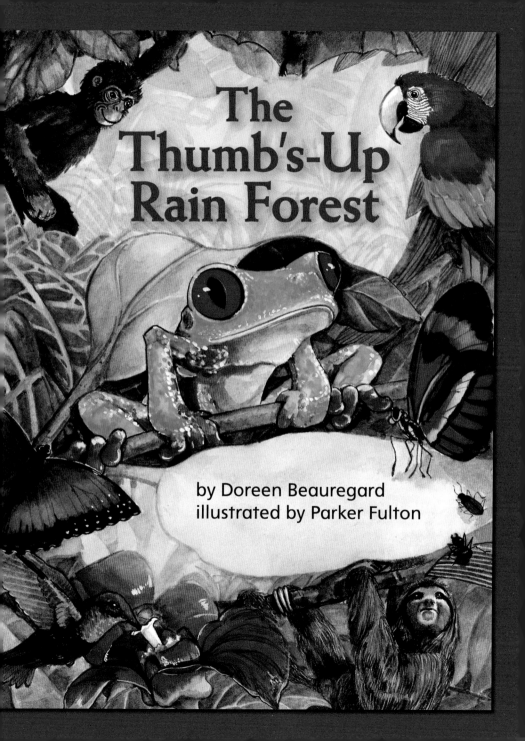

The Thumb's-Up Rain Forest

by Doreen Beauregard
illustrated by Parker Fulton

It is morning in the rain forest. Fran Frog rests in a tree. "I know this rain forest is the very best place to be," Fran says. "I give it a thumbs up!"

"Do my pals like this scene, too?" asks Fran.

Fran asks Bob Bat.

"I like this rain forest. I can hang on this tree limb and sleep all day. I can fly in the sky at night. My mom and dad grew up here, too," says Bob. "This place is just right for me."

Fran asks Abe Ape.

Abe says, "Not a thing is wrong here. I can climb trees and get good food to eat. My friends are very helpful. No one is rude. I will make a sign that says this rain forest is great."

4

Fran asks Pat Parrot.

"This forest has many bright colors. I see gold, red, and green under a blue sky," says Pat. "And I hear wrens making beautiful music. I don't dislike a thing here."

Fran asks April Ant.

April says, "I roam all through this forest. I go from up high to down below. I can smell the fresh scent of flowers on my way. I like all the places in this huge rain forest."

Fran asks Sam Sloth.

"This forest can get hot, but I don't mind the heat. I just go very slowly," says Sam. "I am glad there aren't any gnats to bug me. This place is a great home for me."

Fran clings to a branch with
sticky toes. "I knew it! My friends
like this place as much as I do. We
have lots of food to eat and many
colorful things to see. This is a
thumbs-up rain forest!"

Shirl and Her Tern

by Barbara A. Donovan
illustrated by Barry Ablett

My dad knows a lot about birds.
Each Saturday we find a spot on
Burns Beach to watch them. I like
wrens and terns the best. When terns
swirl in the sky, it's quite a scene. I
would sign up to watch them all day!

Waves churn and gnats cluster
on the beach where the terns feed.
In fall, we feel sad when the terns
fly away.

By last week, we thought the
last tern had flown away. Then, from
the reeds, there was a weak chirp.

11

We turned toward the sound. We moved the reeds and found a tern in the dirt. Something was wrong. The tern was hurt. It didn't stir a bit.

Dad called Fern. She works as an animal doctor. Fern said to bring the bird to the vet building on First Street.

We found a box and used a piece of an old shirt to make a bed. We put the bird in the bed and fed it some crumbs. Then we climbed in the car and drove to see Fern. As we drove, I urged the tern to get well.

Fern checked my tern. She saw
a cut under its wing. Fern got
medicine. She rubbed it on the cut
to kill germs.

Today I got good news. My tern is
fine! In the spring, it will be with the
rest of the terns when they return.

More Fun Than a Hat!

by Mark Melillo
illustrated by Alexandra Willner

When it turns cold outside, how can people keep their ears warm? Pulling on a wool hat works and fixes the problem.

Before wool hats were made, people wrapped long wool scarves around their ears.

Chester Greenwood lived where
the winter winds roar. Chester wore
a wool scarf, but it was itchy. His
bulky scarf made ice-skating a chore.

One day Chester's ears got so sore
they hurt. So Chester made a plan
and got to work.

Chester thought of a way that
was certain to keep his ears warm.
He got a bit of beaver fur, black
velvet, and thin metal strips.

Chester gave these things to his
grandma. She stitched them together.
These were the first earmuffs!

Chester's earmuffs worked. Still, Chester thought they could be better.

A short time later, Chester made changes to his earmuffs. The new earmuffs were easy to carry and weren't heavy. They fit just right.

Soon everyone wanted earmuffs. They started a bit of an uproar.

Chester was just 15 when he came up with this worthwhile plan! In his lifetime he made more useful things.

It was long ago that Chester made the first earmuffs. But in the place where he was born, they still have a party on his birthday.

Cheer Up, Dot

by Liane B. Onish
illustrated by Deborah Melmon

Dot went inside the house.

"What happened, dear?" asked
Mrs. Deer.

"The big kids named me Spots!"
Dot said, with tears dropping from
her big, sad eyes. Then more
tears fell.

This made Mrs. Deer sort of sad.

Mrs. Deer said, "Cheer up, Dot. Each young deer has spots. Here's a tip, dear. Spots can be useful"

So Dot went outside to play again. The deer were bored, so they started a game of Hide and Seek. Fay was It.

Doe stood behind a tree near Fay, but her tail stuck out. Fay found her.

Ray hid behind a bush, but his big horns soared up. Fay found him, too.

Dot lay in the grass. Fay could not spot her, and neither could Doe.

At last, Fay gave up. "Where is Dot? Come here, Dot. You win!" All the deer cheered.

"Here I am!" said Dot, standing up right near them. "I am not gone. I win because of my spots! I like spots!"

Fay said, "Let's wait a year. You will be older and bigger. And you will not have spots. Then we will play again and see who wins at Hide and Seek!"

Dot said, "In a year I may not have spots, but I will be much smarter. I bet I will still win!"

26

The Caring King's Fair Wish

by Jen Roberts
illustrated by Capucine Mazille

Once upon a time, a king lived in a palace. Here the king had a garden filled with rare roses. The king shared his life with his child, Martha.

The king was a fine man. He cared about his people. He had all he could wish for. But still, he wished he had more.

One day the king was in his garden. He was startled there by a man wearing a cloak.

"Why are you here? Where are you going?" asked the king. "Here's my hand. Talk to me."

"I was getting fresh air as I walked among the roses," said the man. " I felt ill and had to rest."

The king took care of the man.
When the man felt well, he went
home. Soon the man came back.

"I can grant wishes," he said. "To
repay you, I will grant you a wish."

"I want all that I touch to turn
to gold!" said the king.

"That's a fair wish," said the man.

The king began to touch things. Soon he had gold chairs, gold stairs, gold rugs, and gold deer!

When he held a pear or a rose, it turned to gold and lost its smell.

At lunch the king's food turned to gold. Scared, the king started to weep big tears.

Martha ran to him. As he patted her hair, she turned to gold!

"Oh, dear. I am sorry," wailed the king. "Now I know that happiness can't be bought with gold."

The man knew how to cheer up the king. He undid the king's wish. And the king was never greedy again.

Unit 4: Our Life/Our World

to use with *Alaska: A Special Place*   **WORD COUNT: 299**

DECODABLE WORDS

Target Phonics Elements

Silent Letters: *wr*
  wrens, wrong

Silent Letters: *kn*
  knew, know

Silent Letters: *gn*
  gnats, sign

Silent Letters: *mb*
  climb, limb, thumbs

Silent Letters: *sc*
  scene, scent

HIGH-FREQUENCY WORDS

below, colors, don't, down, eat, many, morning, sleep, through, very

Review: all, any, are, beautiful, do, flowers, food, for, friends, from, give, good, have, here, of, one, says, there, to, too, under, was

STORY WORDS

forest, hear, parrot

to use with *Into the Sea*   **WORD COUNT: 233**

DECODABLE WORDS

Target Phonics Elements

r-controlled vowel: *er*
cluster, Fern, germs, her, tern, terns, under

r-controlled vowel: *ir*
bird, birds, chirp, dirt, First, Shirl, shirt, stir, swirl

r-controlled vowel: *ur*
Burns, churn, hurt, return, turned, urged

r-controlled vowel: *or*
doctor, works, worst

HIGH-FREQUENCY WORDS

animal, away, building, found, from, Saturday, thought, today, toward, watch

Review: about, all, every, fall, food, for, good, looked, moved, said, sound, their, there, they, to, was, where, would

STORY WORDS

called, car, medicine, something

to use with *Happy New Year*   **WORD COUNT: 210**

DECODABLE WORDS

Target Phonics Elements

r-controlled vowel: *or*

born, short

r-controlled vowel: *ore*

before, chore, more, sore, wore

r-controlled vowel: *oar*

roared, uproar

r-controlled vowel: *ar*

party, scarf, scarves, star, started

HIGH-FREQUENCY WORDS

ago, carry, certain, everyone, heavy, outside, people, problem, together, warm

Review: around, could, how, lived, of, one, pulling, their, to, was, were, where

STORY WORDS

earmuffs, ears, wool

to use with *Sun and Moon*

WORD COUNT: 220

DECODABLE WORDS

Target Phonics Elements

  r-controlled vowel: *eer*

    cheer, cheered, deer

  r-controlled vowel: *ere*

    here, here's

  r-controlled vowel: *ear*

    dear, near, tears, year

HIGH-FREQUENCY WORDS

again, behind, eyes, gone, happened, house, inside, neither, stood, young

Review: all, because, come, could, from, found, have, of, outside, said, to, was, were, what, where, who, you

STORY WORDS

soared, bored

to use with Poetry: *Snow Shape, Nature Walk*   **WORD COUNT: 276**

DECODABLE WORDS

Target Phonics Elements

  r-controlled vowel: *air*
    air, chairs, fair, hair, stairs
  r-controlled vowel: *are*
    care, cared, rare, scared, shared
  r-controlled vowel: *ear*
    pear, wearing
  r-controlled vowel: *ere*
    there, where

HIGH-FREQUENCY WORDS
  among, bought, knew, never, once, soon, sorry, talk, touch, upon
  Review: about, again, all, are, could, food, for, how, lived, of, now, one, people, said, some, to, took, was, you

STORY WORDS
  happiness, palace, walked

HIGH-FREQUENCY WORDS TAUGHT TO DATE

Grade K

a	been	jump	straight	old	how	sky
and	before	knew	sure	beautiful	hundred	small
are	begin	know	their	began	hurt	some
can	below	laugh	then	better	idea	sounds
do	better	learn	there	bird	into	special
for	blue	live	they	blue	isn't	start
go	boy	love	thought	both	know	started
has	brought	make	three	boy	learn	straight
have	build	many	through	buy	leaves	the
he	buy	minutes	today	by	light	their
here	by	more	together	change	like	there
I	call	mother	too	cheer	little	these
is	carry	move	two	climbed	live	they
like	certain	never	under	cold	long	this
little	change	new	until	come	look	those
look	climbed	no	up	could	me	three
me	come	not	upon	country	more	to
my	could	nothing	use	didn't	move	too
play	does	now	very	do	my	took
said	done	of	walked	done	new	try
see	down	old	want	early	now	turned
she	early	once	warm	eight	number	two
the	eat	one	water	either	of	under
this	eight	only	way	even	off	understands
to	enough	open	were	every	often	until
was	every	or	who	fall	on	walk
we	eyes	orange	why	family	one	want
what	fall	other	work	far	only	was
where	father	our	would	few	open	wash
with	find	out	write	field	or	water
you	four	over	yellow	find	orange	were
	friends	people	your	first	other	what
	from	place		five	our	where
Grade I	full	poor	**Grade 2**	flower	out	which
about	funny	pretty	about	food	over	who
across	girl	pull	after	for	part	why
after	give	put	all	friends	picture	without
again	goes	ride	almost	funny	places	won
against	gone	run	also	girl	play	won't
air	good	saw	America	give	pull	work
all	great	says	and	go	put	world
along	grew	school	another	goes	ready	would
also	head	searching	any	good	right	year
always	help	should	apart	great	said	yellow
another	her	shout	are	green	saw	yes
any	house	show	around	group	says	you
around	how	so	baby	grow	school	your
away	instead	some	ball	has	second	
ball	into	soon	because	have	see	
be	it	sound	before	he	seven	
because			begin	hear	she	
				help	should	
				here	show	

DECODING SKILLS TAUGHT TO DATE

CVC letter patterns; short *a*; consonants *b, c, ck, f, g, h, k, l, m, n, p, r, s, t, v;* inflectional ending *-s* (plurals, verbs); short *i*; consonants *d, j, qu, w, x, y, z;* double final consonants; *l* blends; possessives with *'s;* end blends; short *o;* inflectional ending *-ed;* short *e;* contractions with *n't;* *s* blends; *r* blends; inflectional ending *-ing;* short *u;* contractions with *'s;* digraphs *sh, th, ng;* compound words; long *a (a_e),* inflectional ending *-ed* (drop final *e*); long *i (i_e);* soft *c, g, -dge;* digraphs *ch, -tch, wh-, ph;* inflectional ending *-es* (no change to base word); long *e (e_e),* long *o (o_e),* long *u (u_e);* silent letters *gn, kn, wr;* 3-letter blends *scr-, spl-, spr-, str-;* inflectional endings *-ed, -ing* (double final consonant); long *a (ai, ay);* inflectional endings *-er, -est;* long *e (e, ea, ee, ie);* *e* at the end of long *e* words; long *o (o, oa, oe, ow);* 2-syllable words; long *i (i, ie, igh, y);* 2-syllable inflectional endings (changing *y* to *ie*); long *e (ey, y);* inflectional ending *-ed* (verbs; change *y* to *i*); *r*-controlled vowel /ûr/er, ir, ur; inflectional endings *-er, -est* (drop final *e*); *r*-controlled vowel /är/ *ar;* abbreviations Mr., Mrs., Dr.; *r*-controlled vowel /ôr/or, oar, ore; *ea* as short *e;* diphthong /ou/ *ou, ow;* final *e* (mouse, house); diphthong /oi/*oi, oy;* prefixes *re-, un-;* variant vowels /ů /oo, /ü/oo, *ew, ue, u_e, ou;* possessives; variant vowel /ô/a, au, aw, augh; singular and plural possessive pronouns; 2-syllable words; *r*-controlled vowel /âr/*air, are, ear;* contractions; open syllables; closed syllables; final stable syllables; vowel digraph syllables; *r*-controlled vowel syllables; vowel diphthong syllables; short *a, e, i, o, u;* consonant blends *dr, sl, sk, sp, st;* consonant digraphs *ch,-tch, sh, th, wh, ph;* long *a (a_e), i (i_e), o (o_e), u (u_e);* soft *c* and *g;* long *a (a, ai, ay, ea, ei);* consonant blends *scr, spr, str;* long *e (e, ea, ee, ey, ie, y);* prefixes *re-, un-, dis-;* long *i (i, ie, igh, y);* compound words; long *o (o, oa, oe, ow);* inflectional endings *-s, -es;* long *u (ew, u, ue, u_e);* inflectional ending *-ing,* r-controlled vowels *er, ir, ur, ear, eer, ere, ar, or, oar, ore, air, are;* inflectional endings *-er, est;* silent letters *gn, kn, wr, mb;* inflectional ending *-ed;* suffixes *-er, -est;* prefixes *re-, un-, dis-*